CHRISTMAS CRAFTS

Hilary Devonshire, John Lancaster, Lyndie Wright

Consultant: Henry Pluckrose

Photography: Chris Fairclough

FRANKLIN WATTS
New York/London/Sydney/Toronto

Franklin Watts Inc
387 Park Avenue South
New York
NY 10016

Design: K & Co

Editor: Jenny Wood

Printed in Belgium

Library of Congress Cataloging-in-Publication Data
Devonshire, Hilary.
    Christmas crafts / Hilary Devonshire, Lyndie Wright, John,
Lancaster.
        p.   cm. — (Fresh start)
    Summary: Provides step-by-step instructions for making Christmas
decorations, cards, models, and mobiles.
    ISBN 0-531-14073-3
    1. Christmas decorations—Juvenile literature.   2. Handicraft—
—Juvenile literature.   [1. Christmas decorations.   2. Handicraft.]
I. Wright, Lyndie.   II. Lancaster, John, 1930—   III. Title.
TT900.C4D48   1990
745.594'12—dc20   90-32522
                                                         CIP
                                                         AC

Contents

Equipment and materials

This book describes activities which use the following:

Bamboo Sticks
Beads
Brushes for glue and paint
Candles
Candy Wrappers
Cardboard (thick and thin; manilla, white and colored)
Christmas cards (old)
Compass (for drawing circles)
Cotton or nylon thread
Cotton balls
Craft knife
Crayons
Cutting board
Dowel rods
Embroidery thread
Fabric scraps (ribbon, lace, felt, calico)
Felt-tip pens (black and colored, waterproof and water-soluble)
Glue (cold-water paste, Pritt Art Paste, Elmer's white glue)
Jars (old, for water and paste)
Household knife (old)
Magazines
Metallic ink marker pens (gold and silver)
Modeling clay

Needle
Newspapers
Paints — water-based
     — poster
     — tempera
     — acrylic
Paper — textured paper
     — foil paper
     — construction paper
     — colored paper
Paper punch (for making holes)
Pencils (lead and colored)
Ping-pong balls
Plaster of Paris
Plastic food containers (e.g. yogurt pots) in a range of sizes
Rags (old cloths for cleaning)
Ruler (metal, and plastic or wooden)
Saucer or old plate for mixing paints
Saw
Scissors
Shoe boxes (old)
Silver foil
Stamp pads (made from sponge)
Sticky tape
String (or nylon fishing line)
Twigs
Water
Yarn (lengths of 2 or 3 ply)

"Against the feast of Christmas every man's house, also their parish churches were decked with ivy, holly and whatever the season offered to be green. Even the streets were likewise garnished."

This account of Christmas decorations was written over 400 years ago, and the activities which are included in this book have strong links with our historical past. Boys and girls have made Christmas decorations, gifts and cards for many centuries. And of course, in celebrating Christmas, we are celebrating the story of Mary and Joseph and the Christ child born in a stable in Bethlehem almost 2,000 years ago.

Not all our Christmas customs have such a long history. Prince Albert (Queen Victoria's husband) is thought to have introduced the Christmas tree to England in 1841 when he ordered a fir tree to be taken to Windsor Castle and decorated with candles. The fir tree *"ablaze with lighted candles"* was the traditional way in which many people on the mainland of Europe celebrated Christmas. Prince Albert, a German, thought that his children should enjoy the beauty of the tree and experience the excitement of opening the presents which lay beneath it.

The sending of Christmas cards also dates from Victorian times. The custom became very popular in Britain, probably because of the introduction of a postal service (by Roland Hill in 1840) which meant that, for the first time, letters and cards could be sent very cheaply to any address in Great Britain.

We hope you enjoy using this book and that you will have fun making the Christmas Crafts.

The merry time of Christmas
Is drawing very near,
I wish you a happy Christmas
And a happy New Year,
A pocket full of money
A cellar of good cheer
And a fat pig to last you
Till next Christmas be here.

A banner

A paper scroll, or banner, is quite simple to design and make. When completed it can be hung from a rafter or small hook in the ceiling so that it swings gently, or suspended flat against a wall. Either way it should be an effective Christmas decoration.

You may, of course, decide to make two or three scrolls with different messages or designs. If you do decide to make a number of scrolls, then vary their sizes and colors.

You will need a pencil, a ruler, scissors, paper (black, white or colored), glue, a glue brush, a dowel rod (thin sticks or tightly rolled newspaper are useful substitutes), a saw, water-based paints, a paintbrush, a metallic ink marker pen (gold or silver), thin string or nylon fishing line and colored felt-tip pens.

1 Measure then cut out a long, thin rectangle of paper approximately 1½" longer than you wish the finished scroll to be. The example shown here is 4" x 5¾". Paint a strip of glue across each end of the paper.

2 Cut two lengths of dowel rod with the saw. Each one should be 1½" longer than the width of the scroll. Color these with brightly colored paint or with your metallic marker pen. Place one at each end of the paper, above or below the strip of glue, as appropriate.

3 Roll the glued strips over on to the dowel rods, making a loop at each end of the scroll.

4 Make sure the loops are securely fastened. Tie the ends of a length of string around the ends of the top piece of dowel then knot into a single strand. This will enable you to hang up the scroll.

5 Try decorating your scroll by painting a border all the way around the edges. Use strong, bold lines. Add a snow scene in the center or simply paint a colorful pattern of squares, circles or curving lines.

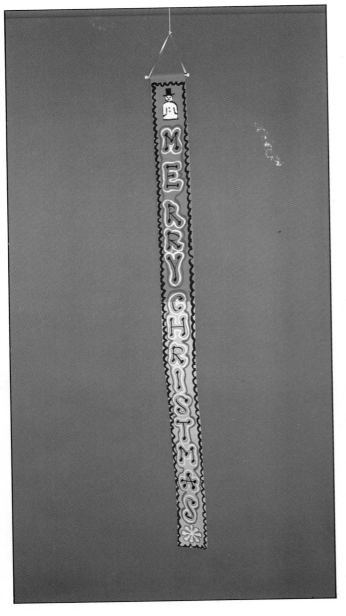

6 Draw MERRY CHRISTMAS in decorated letters down the length of one side of the scroll...

7 ...and HAPPY NEW YEAR on the other side!

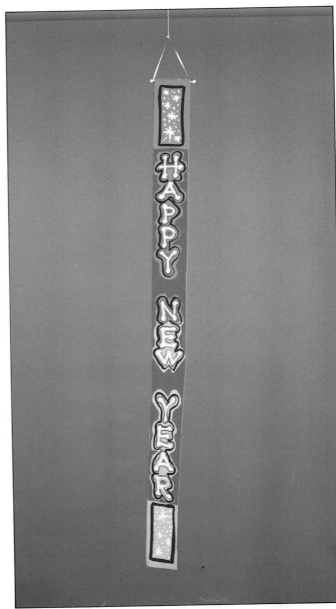

If you want to make a very long scroll which could hang in a stairwell or in a high room, then you will need to attach one or more sheets of paper together. Using different colors of paper will make this look very effective.

A Christmas pyramid

This decorated pyramid is a hanging decoration. Several pyramids dangling from a small hoop can look very attractive.

You will need white cardboard, a pencil, a ruler, scissors, crayons, sticky tape, cotton thread or thin string, glue and a glue brush.

1 On white cardboard and using an equilateral triangle as a template, draw a group of four triangles. They should be positioned exactly as shown in the photograph. Draw a tab along one side of each of the three outside triangles, as shown, then carefully cut out the whole shape. When folded, this will make a pyramid.

2 Draw a picture or pattern on each triangle. This design shows the Three Wise Men and the Star of Bethlehem.

3 Fold the shape along the sides of the center triangle and along the tabs.

4 Using sticky tape, attach a thread to the inside of the pyramid at the top corner of one triangle.

5 Glue each tab and stick the sides of the pyramid together. Hold the edges for a short time while the glue dries.

6 The finished pyramid. What other Christmas designs can you think of?

When we put up paper streamers and other indoor Christmas decorations, we sometimes ignore the windows. Here is an idea for a window decoration.

You will need black or dark-colored paper or thin cardboard, scissors, white poster paint, a paintbrush, a needle, thin cotton or nylon thread, a bamboo stick and thin string or nylon fishing line.

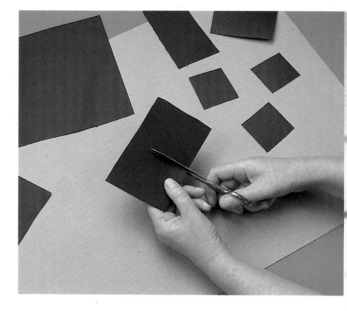

1 Cut a large number of diamond shapes out of the paper or card. Vary the sizes, from about 1½″ square to 4″ square. (The more shapes you produce, the more patterns you will have and the more effective your hanging will become.)

2 Paint a white pattern on both sides of each diamond shape. Vary these patterns, making some of them very simple and delicate, others bolder and more complicated.

3 Using the needle, make a small hole in the top corner of each diamond shape. Cut a length of thread for each shape. Vary the lengths of these threads so that the shapes will hang at different positions. Tie one end of a length of thread through each of the holes.

4 Attach a length of string to each end of the bamboo stick, and knot into a single strand. Hang the diamond shapes from the bamboo, then hang the complete stick from a small hook which should be very near to the top edge of a window.

The finished mobile should, if possible, fill the complete window space.

A "pop-up" Christmas card

This idea has a surprise Christmas message hidden inside the card!

You will need thin white and colored cardboard, felt-tip pens, scissors, a craft knife, a metal ruler and a small piece of ribbon.

1 Draw a Christmas stocking on a piece of colored cardboard 3½″ x 4¼″.

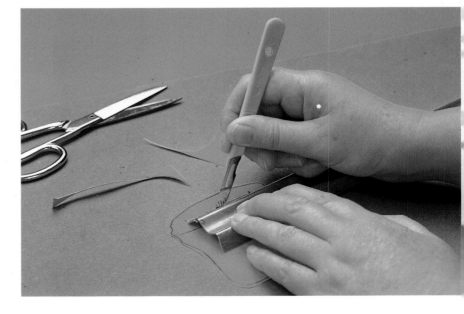

2 Cut out the stocking. Use the craft knife and ruler to make a slit 2″ long near the top.

3 On a piece of white cardboard, draw and color the head and shoulders of a clown. (Your drawing should be about 2″ wide and 3″ high). You will also need a strip of colored cardboard (a different color from the stocking) 2″ wide and 6″ long.

4 Cut out the clown and stick it to the top of the strip of cardboard. Write a secret message underneath.

5 Push the strip of cardboard down through the slit in the Christmas stocking so that the secret message is hidden. Write a message for the front of the Christmas card too, if you like.

6 Fix a short piece of ribbon between the cardboard strip and the stocking so that your Christmas card will stand up.

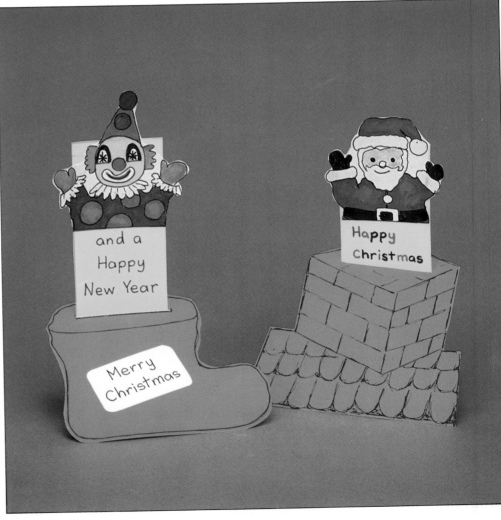

7 Your friends will be surprised when they push up the strip and read the secret message! Why not try some other "pop-up" Christmas card designs?

The front of this Christmas card design is based on the word "NOEL," although you might like to use the word "XMAS" instead. It is a "surprise" card for it has three flaps which, when lifted up, reveal hidden pictures.

You will need thin cardboard or strong paper (any color), a metal ruler, black and colored felt-tip pens or water-based paints, scissors, a craft knife, a cutting board, one or two old Christmas cards, glue and a glue brush.

1 (Left) Measure the shape of your Christmas card (7" x 10") and cut it out. Fold the cardboard in half. Using a black felt-tip pen, draw a rectangle (6¼" x 4¼") on the front face of the folded cardboard so that it has equal borders all around it. Divide this rectangle into four smaller, equal rectangles, then draw a horizontal center line through the two center rectangles.

2 (Left) Draw a large, bold letter "N" in the left-hand rectangle. In two of the center rectangles draw the letters "O" and "E." Then draw a large letter "L" to fill the right-hand rectangle. This completes the word "NOEL."

3 (Above) With brightly colored felt-tip pens or paint, color the letters and background spaces of the Christmas card design.

Making the three flaps

The next step is to make the three surprise flaps. In the example, these are positioned below the letter "O," above the letter "E" and in the space formed to the right of the upward stroke of the letter "L."

4 Place the cardboard on the cutting board. Cut along the sides and bottom edges of these three spaces using the craft knife and metal ruler.

5 Bend the flaps upward. Decorate the spaces beneath the flaps with small pictures of snowmen, Father Christmas, candles, trees, holly and other pictures cut from old Christmas cards.

6 Cut another piece of cardboard or paper 7" x 5" and glue this beneath the design. Remember to leave the flaps unglued.

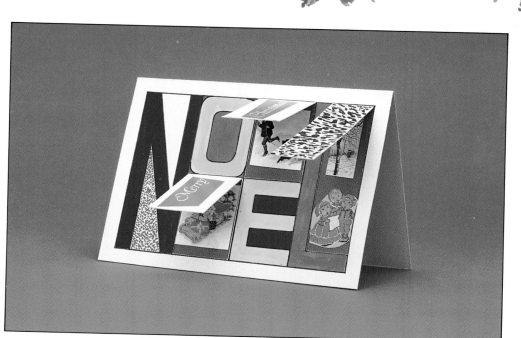

7 The finished card.

8 Add a simple Christmas verse or message to the inside of the card. Either write your own, or cut out the verses from old cards and paste one inside each card you make.

Snowflakes consist of small, usually hexagonal crystals. Here, hexagon shapes are made into a variety of snowflake patterns.

You will need thin white and colored cardboard, a pair of compasses, a pencil, a ruler, glue and a glue brush.

1 Draw a circle, radius 1¾″, on a piece of white cardboard. Mark a point on the edge of the circle.

2 Keeping the compasses open at the same distance (1¾″) and starting at the point you have made on the circle, mark another point further around the edge. Move around the circle in this way until you have six points around the edge.

3 Using the pencil and ruler, join the points to make a hexagon.

4 Cut out your cardboard hexagon, and use it as a template to draw a number of hexagons on white and colored cardboard.

5 Fold each hexagon in half. Now fold over one corner then the opposite corner to make a small triangle shape.

6 Cut out small pieces from the edges of each folded triangle. This is easier if you use thin cardboard.

7 It's great fun unfolding your hexagons and discovering what patterns you have made. Every snowflake is different. Here are some red and white snowflake designs.

8 (Right) You can use your snowflake designs for Christmas cards. Here, a red snowflake pattern is being stuck on to a white hexagon then onto a red card.

9 A selection of snowflake cards. On the left a "see-through" design has been made by sticking a snowflake on to a cut-out hexagonal hole in the card.

The measurements given on the diagram below can be used to help you make envelopes for your Christmas cards. Remember that you can use colored paper.

Envelopes don't have to be white, although the Post Office prefers light colors as the names and addresses are easier to read.

1 The shape of the envelope before gluing.

You will need an old shoe box, a pencil, a ruler, thin white cardboard, poster or tempera paints or crayons, a paintbrush, scissors, glue and a glue brush.

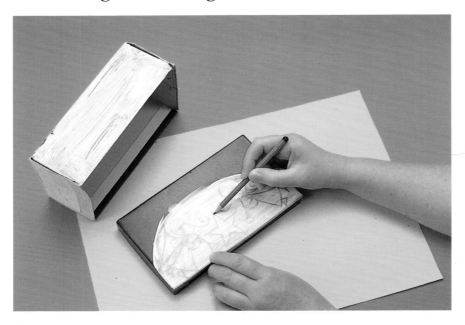

1 The shoe box set on its side will be the stable, and the lid can be used as a sky scene of stars and angels. Start by drawing the stars and angels in the sky.

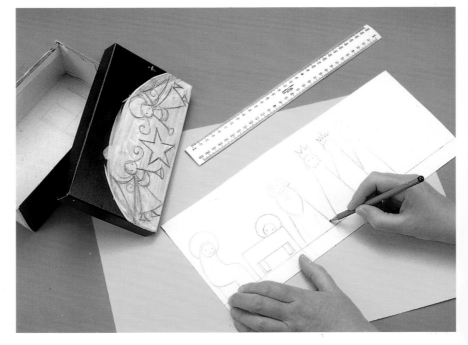

2 Draw the nativity figures on a strip of white cardboard. Measure the box to make sure the figures will fit inside. Leave a blank area about ¾" deep below each figure. This will be folded over and stuck onto the box.

3 Paint or color the figures. Paint the sky scene too, and decorate the inside of the shoe box as a stable (a simple brown wash and a window are quite effective – see photograph **4**).

4 Cut out the painted sky and the figures. Be sure to leave the ¾″ strip at the bottom of each one.

5 Bend back the strip on the base of each figure and glue it to the box base. Glue the sky scene to the top of the box.

6 The finished crib.

You can decorate your Christmas table with small standing figures such as a snowman or Father Christmas.

You will need white cardboard, a pencil, a pair of compasses, a ruler, scissors, felt-tip pens, glue and a glue brush.

1 On a piece of cardboard draw a small circle with a radius of ¾" for the head. Using the same center point, draw a larger semi-circle (hold the ruler in position to give you the base line). This will be the body. Cut out the complete shape.

2 Use the card outline as a template. Draw around the shape on another piece of white cardboard and add a face and hat as well as arms and hands. Color your figure with felt-tip pens. This snowman has a red and green walking stick and blue eyes.

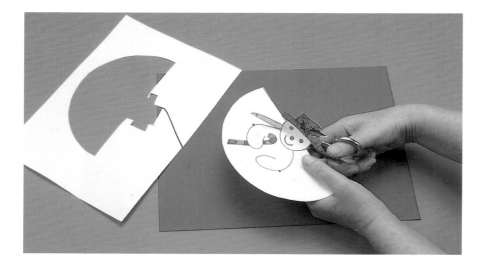

3 Cut out your figure. Cut carefully along the sides of the face and down the arms to the elbows.

4 Fold the body into a cone shape and glue the edges together at the back of the figure.

5 The finished figures. The Father Christmas in the center has been made from red foil paper and decorated with cotton balls.

You will need three sheets of paper (each one a different color), a pair of compasses, a pencil, scissors, felt-tip pens or silver and gold metallic ink marker pens, Elmer's glue, a ping-pong ball and a craft knife.

1 Take one sheet of paper and, using the compasses, draw a circle 4¾" in radius. Cut around the circle and cut a line from the edge to the center. You will know where the center is by the hole made by the compass point.

2 Carefully cut a small hole about ⅜" across at the center of the circle. Draw a pattern on half of the circle, using the felt-tip or metallic marker pens. This will be the fairy's skirt.

3 Carefully bend the circle to form a cone about 3½" across at the base. Glue the edges together. Make sure the skirt pattern is on the outside!

4 Take another sheet of paper (a different color this time) and fold it in half. Draw and cut out a pair of wings, then decorate them with the felt-tip or metallic marker pens.

5 Take the ping-pong ball and cut a small hole (about ³⁄₈″ across) with the craft knife. (You may need an adult to help with this.) Put a little glue around the edge of the hole and stick the ball onto the cone.

6 Glue the wings in position, too.

7 Fold a scrap of paper the same color as the skirt and cut out a simple pair of arms. Decorate these and glue them onto the cone.

8 Cut out a star for the fairy to hold and glue it in position. Draw a face on the ping-pong ball.

9 To make the hair, take a small piece of paper (a third color, if possible). Cut strips at both ends and leave an uncut bit in the center. If you would like your fairy to have curly hair, roll the strips around the end of the pencil.

10 Your fairy is now complete and ready for the Christmas tree!

Cover yourself with an apron and your table or work surface with old newspapers before you try out this idea!

You will need Plaster of Paris ("finishing" or dental plaster is best), plastic containers to use as molds, an old plastic container for mixing the plaster, candles, Modeling clay, water, an old household knife, a piece of cloth, poster or acrylic paint and a paintbrush.

1 A collection of different-shaped containers which you can use as candle-holder molds.

2 Select a mold and fasten a candle to it. Use modeling clay to hold the candle firmly in position. You don't want it falling over when you pour the plaster around it!

3 Pour into your mixing container as much water as would fill your mold. Slowly and evenly sprinkle Plaster of Paris into the water. Start at the outer edges of the mixing container and work toward the center. Continue adding plaster until you are left with a dry island of plaster in the center. Don't *mix* the plaster yet.

4 Now, working quickly, mix the plaster with your hands. Make sure it is lump-free!

5 When it reaches a creamy consistency it is about to set, so pour it into the mold at once. Now wash and dry your hands. Be careful not to get plaster down the drain as it could cause a blockage.

6 When the plaster is no longer runny, carefully remove the candle from the mold.

7 Wait about ten minutes, then take the plaster shape out of the mold. You may need to cut the mold to get the plaster out.

8 Using the old knife, cut patterns into the plaster shape. This is great fun to do, but take your time! It would be a pity to spoil your candle holder at this stage. Rub the crumbs of plaster off with an old cloth.

9 When dry, paint the carved shape with poster or acrylic paint.

10 A collection of candle holders, each one a different shape and design.

Some trees and bushes still have their leaves at Christmas, so you can use these to make a decorative centerpiece for your Christmas dinner table.

You will need a piece of cardboard, modeling clay, silver foil, white paint, a paintbrush, some twigs (with leaves on), and small hanging decorations.

1 Shape some modeling clay on a piece of cardboard as a base for the twigs.

2 Cover the modeling clay with silver foil. Paint the leaves and twigs with some white paint to look like snow. The ones shown here are from a laurel bush. Push the twigs into the modeling clay.

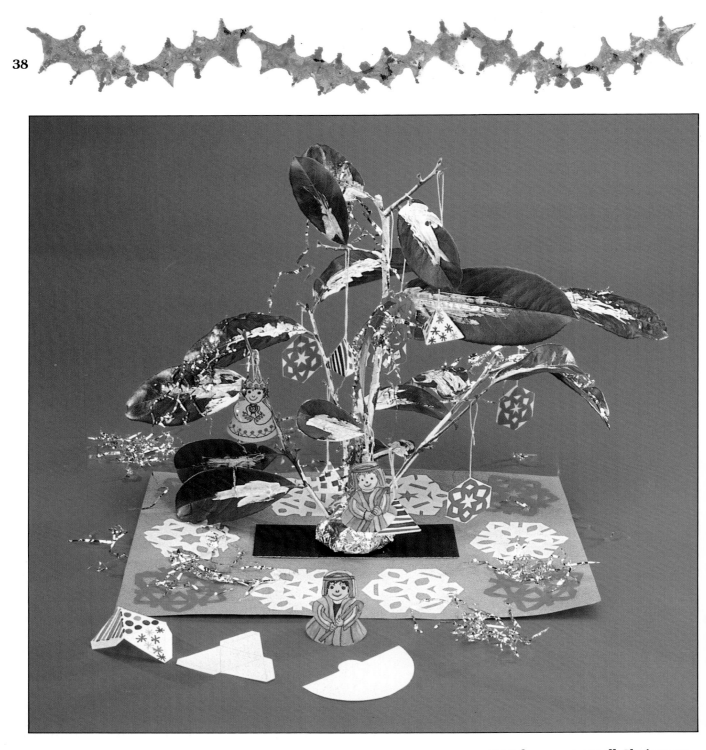

3 Make some small Christmas decorations to hang on the twigs. You can use some ideas from this book – for example, miniature figures (pp 27-28), pyramids (pp 9-11), and snowflakes (pp 20-22). You can even make a table mat for your decoration to stand on.

A Christmas print

You can make sponge prints of many Christmas shapes and patterns. Here a robin is used to make a Christmas picture.

You will need a thin sponge, a pen, scissors, cardboard, glue, a glue brush, paints, a paintbrush and white and colored paper.

1 Draw a robin, or another shape of your choice, on the sponge and cut it out.

2 Glue the sponge robin on to the cardboard. Leave to dry. Fill the sponge with paint, letting the paint soak in.

3 Make a print on white paper. Experiment to see how much paint you need to get a good print.

4 The finished design. The black paper background was textured by printing with a scrap of sponge and white paint. Holly leaves have been printed in a circle around the robin.

Bookmarks

Bookmarks are useful Christmas gifts for friends and relatives. They are attractive and easy to make.

You will need some stiff paper or cardboard (white, black or colored), a pencil, a ruler, scissors, a paper punch, colored scrap paper (e.g. magazines, candy wrappers, silver foil), glue, a glue brush, felt-tip pens and colored ribbon (thin) or string.

1 Draw a number of rectangles on the paper or cardboard then cut them out carefully. A good size for each is 2″ x 9¾″. Punch a small hole in the center of each card near to the bottom edge.

2 Cut a number of diamond shapes in varying sizes from the colored scrap paper. Glue these diamonds on to the front of your bookmark. Make some of them overlap so that the design is more interesting.

3 Another idea is to draw a border around the edge of the bookmark with a black felt-tip pen. Fill in the space in the middle with circles, drawn freehand. These can overlap or touch, and you may vary them in size. Color in your design.

4 Complete the bookmark by adding a colorful tail. Take one or two lengths of colored ribbon or string and pull them through the hole near the bottom edge of the bookmark. Put a touch of glue at the back to hold them in place.

5 The finished bookmark.

Finger puppets and stage

You will need calico, water-soluble felt pens, a paintbrush, scissors, a needle and thread, embroidery thread, yarn, felt, beads, and bits of lace for decoration. For the stage you will need an old shoe box, a craft knife, a metal ruler, a pencil, tempera or poster paints and a paintbrush.

1 Place your finger on a folded piece of calico and draw around it. Draw a dotted line ⅜″ away. Draw a third line, a solid line, ⅜″ away from the dotted line. This third line you have drawn will be the cutting line. Cut out the finger puppet shape.

2 Sew along the dotted line using small running stitches. Finish off securely with a few stitches on top of each other. When you have done this, turn the shape inside out.

3 It may help to iron the calico shape before you start to color it. Draw the puppet using water-soluble felt pens. These allow you to wash or fade the colors into each other. Experiment on a scrap of material first.

4 When the color has dried, decorate the puppet with embroidery thread or yarn for hair, a felt hat, bead eyes, a lace collar or whatever you choose. You can make as many finger puppets as you like.

5 An old shoe box on end makes a very good stage for the finger puppets. Draw a rectangle in the bottom of the box. Using the craft knife and metal ruler, cut along three sides of this rectangle, leaving the upper side attached – this piece may be lifted up and used as a curtain.

6 Paint the box to look like a Punch and Judy booth. Your stage is ready for the puppets to give their show!

Most of the materials mentioned in this book are easy to obtain. Some are simply scrap materials and will cost you nothing. Others, such as paints, felt-tip pens, cardboard and adhesives, can be purchased from stationers and/or artists' materials shops.

Brushes

Use white hog-hair brushes, which are hard-wearing and comparatively cheap. Sizes 6, 8 and 12 are recommended for the activities included in this book (size 6 for small-scale work, size 12 for large-scale work).

Wax crayons

Good quality wax crayons are made in a wide range of colors (including gold, silver and bronze) and thicknesses. They are obtainable from shops that sell artists' materials and from some stationers and variety stores.

Paper

If you want to get a range of papers, both hand-and machine-made, you will find the following suppliers useful:

Triarco Arts & Crafts
14650 28th Ave. North
Plymouth, MN 55441
612-559-5590
800-328-3360

Sax Arts & Crafts
P.O. Box 2002
Milwaukee, WI 53201
414-272-4900
1-800-242-4911

Dick Blick Art Materials
P.O. Box 1267
Galesburg, Il 61401
309-343-6181
1-800-447-8192

A.I. Friedman, Inc.
Art and Drafting Materials
25 W 45th Street
New York, NY 10036
212-575-0200

J.L. Hammett
P.O. Box 545
Braintree MA 02184